Atka's Ice Adventure

Written by Max Greenslade

Illustrated by Meredith Thomas

Flying Start
to Literacy®

T0342927

Contents

Chapter 1:
Footprints in the snow

Atka was half asleep. It was nighttime, but the sun was still high in the sky. Her little sister, Nukka, was fast asleep beside her.

Atka could hear Father and
Grandfather talking.

"Our friend Olaf had a lucky escape,"
said Father.

"What happened?" asked Grandfather.

"He was fishing out on the sea ice. The ice
broke away from the land and drifted out
to sea," said Father. "But luckily he drifted
back when the tide changed. And that's
when he saw polar bear cubs."

Polar bear cubs! Now Atka was wide awake.
She wanted to see polar bear cubs more
than anything, but the only place you
could see them was out on the sea ice.

But, when she asked Father and Grandfather
if she could go fishing with them on the
sea ice, they said no, it was too dangerous.

The next morning, everyone was busy doing chores. Father and Grandfather were busy mending the kayak. Mother was putting the fish on the drying rack. Atka watched Nukka play and sing.

Atka was thinking about the polar bear and her cubs. She started to make a cub out of snow. She pinched the snow into little ears. Now what could she use for eyes?

She looked around, and that's when she realised that Nukka had stopped singing. Atka couldn't see Nukka anywhere, but she could see her footprints in the snow.

Without thinking, Atka followed Nukka's footprints out over the snow ridge, away from the camp. In the distance, she could see Nukka.

Atka started to run. What if Nukka went out on the sea ice and it broke up and drifted away?

"Stop, Nukka!" shouted Atka.
"It's dangerous out there."

But Nukka couldn't hear her.

Chapter 2:
A crack in the ice

Finally, Atka reached Nukka just as she got to the sea ice.

"Oh, Nukka," she said, "we have to get back to camp. We shouldn't be out here by ourselves."

But it was too late. Suddenly, there was a loud cracking sound. The ice that Atka and Nukka were standing on began to crack and drift away from the land.

Nukka screamed and ran towards
the edge of the ice floe.

"No," said Atka. "Stay back.
We might fall into the sea."

Nukka started to cry. Atka put her
arms around her. The ice floe drifted
rapidly out to sea. Atka tried not to
show that she was frightened.

Atka knew very well the dangers of the sea ice. Large sheets of ice could break off and become ice floes. The ice floes could float out to sea.

She remembered the story that Father had told about Olaf. It had happened to him. But the ice floe had floated back to the land when the tide changed and he had just walked off.

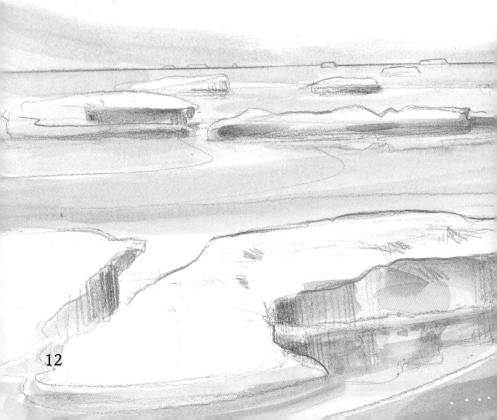

"We will float back to the land soon,"
said Atka.

But, as they floated out into the icy blue
ocean, Atka was afraid. She was so afraid
that she had a lump in her throat.

Chapter 3:
Polar bear! Polar bear!

Suddenly, Nukka called out,
"Polar bear! Polar bear!"

Atka saw something move in the distance –
it was a polar bear!

Atka couldn't believe her luck. It was
the first polar bear she had ever seen.
Were there any cubs?

Atka looked hard, but she could see only the polar bear, no cubs.

Suddenly, the polar bear lifted its nose to sniff the air. It could smell Atka and Nukka. Then the polar bear started to walk towards the edge of the ice floe. It was walking towards them!

Atka knew that polar bears swam between ice floes to hunt. She didn't feel so brave anymore.

"Oh, help!" she cried.

Chapter 4:
Just in time

Suddenly, the polar bear stopped.
In the distance, there was the sound
of shouting and dogs barking.

Someone was coming – they would be rescued. It was their family!

When Father and Grandfather reached the sea, they quickly put the kayak in the water. Father got in the kayak and paddled fast towards them.

"Stay back from the edge!" he shouted.

Father used the paddle to stay close to the ice floe, while Atka and Nukka carefully got into the kayak. He pushed away from the ice floe and paddled back to shore.

"I'm sorry, Father," said Atka. "I should not have left the camp without telling you, but I had to go after Nukka."

Atka thought that Father and Grandfather would be angry with her. But they weren't.

"You saved your sister's life," said Father.

"You were very brave," said Grandfather. "It's dangerous out here on the sea ice, but you knew what to do."

"You can come fishing with us next time," said Father.

Atka was very happy. She looked out over the sea ice one last time and that's when she saw them – polar bear cubs! There were two of them, and they were with their mother!

They all watched as the mother polar bear stopped and sniffed the air again.

Atka turned to her father.
"Can we come back soon?"

A note from the author

I once watched an old documentary about an indigenous family in the Arctic. They were building an igloo to sleep in. The documentary showed the many dangers for indigenous people in the Arctic: travelling, hunting for food, and even fishing.

As I watched the children play in the snow, I wondered how they learned about the dangers of the snow and ice, and the polar bears.

In *Atka's Ice Adventure*, I wanted to show some of these dangers. In the story, Atka is rewarded for listening and remembering what to do when faced with a danger.